ALL CORDOBA

Text, photographs, design, lay-out and printing, entirely created by the technical department of EDITORIAL ESCUDO DE ORO, S.A.

Rights of total or partial reproduction and translation reserved.

3rd Edition

I.S.B.N. 84-378-1776-5

Dep. Legal B. 7368-1998

Editorial Escudo de Oro, S.A.

◁ *19th-century engraving of the mosque.*

The Roman bridge over the Guadalquivir and the Albolafia mill.

HISTORY OF THE CITY

Córdoba is a city rich in art and history, its origins going back to ancient times. However, the date of its foundation as a city is placed between the years 169 and 152 BC, when Claudius Marcellus installed a Roman colony here due to its privileged position as a riverport on the Guadalquivir and entranceway to the entire region of Andalusia. Converted into the capital of Hispania Ulterior, Córdoba was a Roman city for eight centuries, flourishing as a trading centre whose prestige was increased by its great poets and philosophers, including Seneca and Lucan.

The Moorish invasion of the city took place in the year 711, though more than a conquest this entailed the surrender of Córdoba based on an agreement under which the life and religious beliefs of its inhabitants were to be respected. Thus began a new period of prosperity during which three cultures and religions, the Moorish, the Hebrew and the Christian, lived peacefully side by side. Five years after occupying the city, the Moors converted Córdoba into the capital of Al-Andalus and in the year 756, after a bloody struggle between the Omeyas and the Abasidas, the then Prince Abderramán took over the reigns of power, creating an independent Emirate, no longer recognising the religious supremacy of Baghdad. Two centuries later, in the year 929, Abderramán III proclaimed the Caliphate of Córdoba, thus achieving complete independence.

Under Moorish rule, Córdoba enjoyed its period of maximum splendour, becoming famed as the most

The Roman bridge.

The Puerta del Puente, Triunfo de San Rafael, The Roman bridge and the Torre de la Calahorra. ▷

flourishing city and the cultural capital of the Western world, with a magnificent university, fabulous libraries and sumptuous buildings such as the aljama mosque and the Medina Azahara. Its population was over one million, and Moorish sources record 1,600 mosques in the city. However, by the year 1013 internecine strife had brought about the dismemberment of the caliphate, and a Reign of Taifas (small kingdoms) was installed, Córdoba coming to depend on that of Seville. This political decadence did not affect intellectual development in the city, however, as is

Night-time view of the cathedral.

Aerial view of the cathedral-mosque, adjoining which are the labyrinthine streets of the Jewish quarter.

demonstrated by such illustrious sons as the poet Aben Hazam, the philosopher Averroes and the Jewish doctor and thinker Maimonides.

In 1236, Córdoba was reconquered by the Christian army of Ferdinand III, the Holy, and it was incorporated into the Kingdom of Castile. Its caliphal splendour lost, from this time on until the end of the 19th century, Córdoba was considered a mere «city of transit». In the 20th century, however, its importance increased once more as the city was modernised to provide a complete range of services and was established as a key point in communications between the south of Spain and the rest of Europe. Córdoba now has a population of around 315,000, and is no longer a «city of transit». Around its historic centre, one of the largest in Europe, declared patrimony of humanity by UNESCO in 1994, are wide avenues and peaceful parks and gardens which, joined to the pleasant climate of the region, make this an attractive, inviting and evocative city.

The Fuente del Olivo in the Patio de los Naranjos and the cathedral belltower.

Entrance in the western front of the mosque, built during the reign of Alhakem II (10th century).

The Puerta del Perdón in the north side, features three horseshoe arches.

The Chapel of the Virgen de los Faroles and belltower, in the north side of the cathedral-mosque site.

The east and south fronts of the mosque.

THE MOSQUE

The Mosque and Cathedral is the symbol of the period of maximum splendour of Córdoba. It is also an example of the overlaying of civilisations which has occurred here. The monument we see today is a heterogeneous building consisting of two very different oratories. As a mosque, it is the largest in the Western World, with a total area of almost 24,000 m². It is, moreover, along with such monuments as the Medina Azahara Palace, one of the world's most important exponents of what is known as Caliphal art. The exterior of the mosque comprises an imposing crenellated wall, frequently reinforced by square tur-

Arches of the maqsura and the doorway of the mihrab.

Doorway of the mihrab.

rets and containing a large number of gates. In the north side, which also features the tower, are the Puerta del Perdón and the so-called «Caño Gordo». The Puerta del Perdón dates back to the 14th century and is in impeccable Mudéjar style. Its name («Gate of Pardon») derives from the fact that was here that, on feast days, the Chapter released its debtors from their obligations. Adjoining the «Caño Gordo» is a small altar to the Virgen de los Faroles, which acquires a particular charm at night, when it is illuminated. The outstanding gates on the west wall are the Gothic «Postigo de la Leche» («Gate of the Milk»), thus-known because it was here that foundlings were left to the care of the Chapter; and the San Esteban and San Miguel gates, decorated in Caliphal style. In the east side, two fine gates give access to the Patio de los Naranjos, and the wall also features the Renaissance-style Puerta de Santa Catalina and another, nameless, in Churrigueresque style.

The Patio de los Naranjos, as this courtyard has been known since the Christian reconquest, when it was planted with orange trees, is most splendid in spring, when it is full of the sweet smell of blossom. In Moorish times, this the place where the faithful washed before entering the mosque, whilst the galleries surrounding it were the place of prayer for women. In the centre is the Aljibe de Almanzor, which dates back to the 10th century, whilst next to the Puerta del Perdón rises the tower. This was the first great minaret to be built in Spain, and dates back to the times of Abderramán III, though restoration in the 16th century concealed its original structure. In the 17th century, it was lined with stone in order to strengthen it, and two new sections were added. At the top is a statue of Saint Raphael, by Pedro de Paz. From the belltower, the visitor commands splendid panoramic views over the city.

The mosque was formerly reached from this courtyard via a number of arches, but these have since been closed up, as in the 17th century the different chapels were established on the other side of them. The only exception is the Puerta de las Palmas, also known as the «Arch of Blessings», due to the fact that it was here that the standards of armies engaged in the reconquest of Granada were blessed. It is through here that we can gain access to the original mosque, built under Abderramán I.

After Cordova had fallen to the Moors in the year 711, the conquerors shared the Visigoth Church of San Vicente with the Christian population. This church occupied the site of what is now the mosque, and where it is thought that a Roman temple dedicated to the Sun once stood.

The church was soon made too small by the rapid

The horseshoe arch giving access to the mihrab is adorned with Byzantine mosaics.

Dome in the antechamber to the mihrab.

The central dome in the mihrab is of outstanding beauty.

expansion of the city's population at this time, and in the year 786 Abderramán I bought the Christian section, after which a splendid mosque was erected in a matter of just a few years.

The original mosque consisted of 11 longitudinal and 12 transversal aisles. At the end of the central aisle or nave, in the qibla, or wall facing Mecca, was the mihrab. On the north side, the main front of the building, was a wall containing arches which communicated with the washing area, in which courtyard was built a first minaret. The mosque was constructed using columns, capitals and stone from Roman and Visigoth buildings in Spain, Europe and even Africa,

The stone shell forming the dome of the mihrab.

making this early section a veritable archaeological museum exhibiting a diversity of capitals, as well as splendid marble.

The arches, Moorish on the lower level and semicircular above, are Visigoth in style and are formed by voussoirs in red brick and white stone, giving the site a peculiar bichromatic effect. The arches were superimposed in order to heighten and lighten the building and to make it possible to illuminate it from the courtyard. This innovative element seems to have taken its inspiration from the construction methods used in Roman aqueducts. The aisles were covered with wooden coffering, whilst the floor, originally beaten earth covered with mats, was laid in marble during the 19th century.

Due to the constantly increasing population of the city, the mosque was successively extended until it took the form in which we now see it. The first extension (833-852) was carried out by Abderramán II, and was the section most affected later by the construction of the cathedral. Alhakem II undertook the second, which took from 961 to 966 to complete,

The naves of Alhakem II are characterised by polyfoiled arches.

A view of the Capilla Real, built in pure Mudéjar style. ▷

Arcades of Alhakem II.

and the third extension, in 987, is the work of Almanzor. This last was the most solemn of all, and almost double the total area of the mosque. In all, there were 1,013 columns here, of which 856 survived the reforms carried out to integrate the various Christian churches. The Alhakem II extension is the richest of all, and is considered a fine exponent of Caliphal art. Besides the mihrab, which deserves mention apart, the outstanding features of this section are the cusped arches forming the entrance and boundaries to it, and the Patio de Columnas, a «courtyard of columns» characterised by its alternating colours, with simple Corinthian capitals in the blue marble shafts and compound capitals in those of red marble.

The mihrab is, both architecturally and decoratively, a work of stunning beauty and fantasy. The maxura (area reserved for the Caliph) or antechamber is composed of three chapels, each with its dome-shaped skylight, decorated with mosaic, of which the perfect geometrical progression of that of the central chapel is particularly fine. From it formerly hung a monumental silver lamp, richly-adorned and bearing a host of lamps of perfumed oil. The right-hand chapel led to a corridor along which the caliph entered the mosque directly from the palace, whilst the left-hand chapel gave access to the treasure chamber, where the liturgical objects and donations to the mosque were kept. The mihrab, a small niche of octagonal groundplan, is crowned by a shell-shaped dome made from a single block of marble.

The intertwining arches of the maqsura or mihrab antechambere.

Arch giving entrance to the maqsura.

A forest of columns forming part of the extension carried out by Almanzor.

After the reconquest of the city in 1236 by King Ferdinand III, the Holy, the Bishop of Osma respected the construction inherited, merely consecrating the mosque as a cathedral, giving it the name of Santa María la Mayor and placing a Christian cross over the minaret. In 1254, however, the first Christian church was built within the site, the Chapel of San Clemente, of which only one portal survives. Later, up to the 16th century, successive alterations were carried out to adapt the mosque to Christian worship, with decoration which harmonised with the rest of this monumental building and conserving the overall design of the mosque. These reforms include the construction of the Capilla Real and the Chapel of Villaviciosa.

The Capilla Real was built in 1258 by order of King Alphonse X and was originally intended to serve as his burial place, though it finally became the sacristy of the Chapel of Villaviciosa. It is characterised by its decoration in Mudéjar plasterwork, reminiscent of the Nasarite art of Granada. The Chapel of Villaviciosa dates to the late-15th century and features a splendid dome. It formerly contained the statue of the Virgin of Villaviciosa, now installed in the high altar of the cathedral.

Visigoth altar and Caliphal font.

Arcades of Alhakem II. ▷

The naves of Alhakem II converge on the rear section of the cathedral's high altar.

Chapel of Villaviciosa.

Altarpiece in the Chapel of San José.

Choir and high altar. ▷

THE CATHEDRAL

The construction of the cathedral, or Capilla Mayor, in the very centre of the Moorish mosque began in 1523 at the proposal of Bishop Alonso Manrique, not without controversy, due to the strong opposition led by chief magistrate Luis de la Cerda and aimed at saving the original work. The king's authorisation for the new building had finally to be sought, though, some years later, passing through the city, he visited the mosque for the first time and expressed his regret for the decision taken in his name. Leaving aside questions of appropriateness, however, the overall result is of considerable interest.

The cathedral was designed by Hernán Ruiz, his son, Juan de Ochoa and Diego de Praves. Though originally conceived as a Gothic work, the influence of other architectural styles such as the Mudéjar, Plateresque and Isabelline, can be seen in it. Its outstanding features include the fine choirstalls by Pedro Duque Cornejo (18th century). Carved in mahogany from the Indies, these depict scenes from the Old and New Testaments, the life of the Virgin Mary and that of various Cordoban martyrs. Also baroque

in style are the pulpits, carved by Michel de Verdiguier. Over the centre of the crossing are enormous silver lamps by Martín Sánchez de la Cruz. The altarpiece, made from Carcabuey marble, features paintings by Antonio de Palomino and gilt wooden carvings by Pedro de Paz.

Separate from this elements, to the left of the *qibla*, is the Sacristy, also known as the Chapel of Santa Teresa. This was built in 1703 and contains the tomb of its founder, Pedro de Salazar, cardinal and bishop of Córdoba. The magnificent cathedral treasure is reached trough one of the side doors here. The many pieces displayed here include the Arfe Monstrance, a splendid example of the silverwork of Enrique Arfe representing a Gothic cathedral more than two metres in height. The monstrance has led the Corpus Cristi processions each year since 1518.

Adjoining the Chapel of Santa Teresa, in the east wall, is a *Last Supper* by Pedro de Céspedes (16th century). Nearby is an independent altar in Mudéjar style featuring an *Annunciation* by Pedro de Córdoba painted in the 14th century.

*Door of
San
Jacinto.*

City walls and the monument to Averroes.

THE CITY WALLS

Near to the gardens of the Alcázar are the ruins of the old Almoravide walls, almost 400 metres in length, around six metres high and over two metres thick. Various towers survive, some of them in near ruinous state, and many of the old city gates have also been destroyed over the centuries. Nevertheless, a few can still be admired, such as the 10th-century Puerta de Sevilla, with its two identical arches, or the Puerta de Almodóvar, possibly first built in the 14th century, though restored in the 19th. Facing the Puerta de Sevilla is the statue honouring the Cordoban poet Aben Hazam (994-1064), whilst next to the walls is that of Averroes (1126-1198), the Moorish philosopher, born in Córdoba, who introduced Aristotelian thought to the Western world. Another illustrious son of the city is Seneca (4 BC to 65 AD), a monument to whom adjoins the Puerta de Almodóvar.

EL ALCAZAR DE LOS REYES CRISTIANOS

This royal residence of the Christian Monarchs began to be built in 1328 at the behest of Alphonse XI, the Just. During the Moorish period and, possibly, during the Roman occupation, this site was used for military purposes. It was later extended with the introduction of parks and gardens, and was reformed by the Catholic Monarchs, who used it as their residence whilst they directed the final military operations, culminating in the reconquest of Granada. Here, too, the Catholic Monarchs received Columbus. After the surrender of Granada, they gave it to the Courts of the Holy Office, which occupied it until the abolition of the Inquisition in 1821. It was later used as a military and civil prison until, in 1951 it passed into the possession of the city council, which restored it to its original character as a medieval palace.

The building has a square groundplan, its thick walls, dotted with lookout posts and loopholes, featuring four towers communicated by sentry paths: the Torre del Río, cylindrical in shape; the octagonal keep, Gothic in style; that of Los Leones, Mudéjar; and that of La Vela, rebuilt in 1981. The Alcázar contains many extraordinary archaeological treasures, including 1st and 2nd century Roman sarcophagi and an important collection of mosaics, also Roman. The Moorish baths, built during the days of the Caliphate, are well-preserved, as is the so-called «Patio Morisco». Nevertheless, the main attraction of the Alcázar resides in its splendid gardens in which, as is traditional in Moorish gardens, water, in the form of fountains and ponds, is a key protagonist.

Monument to the poet Ibn-Hazm in the Puerta de Sevilla.

A view of the gardens of the Alcázar de los Reyes Cristianos, showing the way they are arranged in terraces. The pools and exuberant vegetation make these gardens ideal for a quiet walk.

Views of the Alcázar
gardens.

Monument to Alphonse X,
the Wise, in the Alcázar
gardens.

Puerta de Almodóvar and the monument to Seneca.

Entrance to the synagogue in Calle Judíos.

THE SYNAGOGUE

The synagogue, according to an inscription, was built in 1314 by the architect Isaac Majeb. It is, along with two others in Toledo, the only one from these times to have survived in Spain. It served its original purpose until 1492, year of the expulsion of the Jews, and was later used as a rabies hospital and after 1588 belonged to the shoemakers' guild, during which time a chapel dedicated to the patron saint of shoemakers, Saint Crispin, was added. Towards the end of the 19th century, its origins as a Hebrew temple were discovered mortar covering its walls was removed, and it was declared a national monument.

The walls of the synagogue are decorated in rich plasterwork.

Situated in Calle Judíos, close to Plazuela de Maimonides, in the heart of the Jewish quarter, the entrance to the synagogue is through a small patio. In the vestibule which serves as an antechamber is the staircase to the upper floor, with toothed arches, where women were allowed to attend services. The tiny prayer room, square in shape, is decorated with fine plasterwork featuring floral and geometrical motifs, as well as inscriptions from the Hebrew Psalms in a clearly Mudéjar style. The east wall contains an opening for the tabernacle, where the scrolls of the pentateuch (the first five books of the Old Testament) were kept.

The monument to Maimonides, in Calle Judíos.

THE JEWISH QUARTER

This is a medieval quarter of strong architectural personality, a veritable labyrinth of narrow, winding little streets of great charm and beauty, making it one of the most popular tourist attractions in the city. It is also one of the largest and best-preserved such quarters in the world, maintaining its peculiar physiognomy and, in short, its atmosphere and picturesque quality. Its streets, containing fascinating historic buildings and pleasant nooks and corners, spreads out around the mosque, stretching out to the old city walls. One of the main entrance to the Jewish quarter is, in fact, through the Puerta de Almodóvar.

Arco del Portillo.

Plaza de la Corredera.

THE CITY

To walk around Córdoba is to note constantly, throughout this monumental city, the marks of centuries of history and art. The principal Roman works here are the bridge and the temple. The Roman Temple, in Calle Claudio Marcelo, dates to the 1st century BC. Its columns, much restored, originally made up a huge place of worship dedicated to the gods of mythology. The Roman Bridge, also known as the Puente Viejo, formed part of the old Via Augusta, though only the foundations remain from this period. This was for centuries, along with the Puerta del Puente, the southern entrance to Córdoba. Though in Roman times there stood here a triumphal arch, the Puerta del Puente as we see it now was designed by Hernán Ruiz III in 1571 on the occasion of Philip II's visit to the city.

Both the bridge and the Puerta del Puente feature statues of Saint Raphael, guardian angel of the city. Popular devotion for the archangel dates back to the 16th century when, according to legend, Raphael appeared to a clergyman, promising him that the city was in his custody. Most of the monuments to Saint Raphael, whose image appears again and again throughout Córdoba, date to the 17th and 18th centuries and are known as *triunfos* («triumphs») in allusion to the glory of the archangel. The Triunfo de San Rafael found near the Puerta del Puente, by French artist Michel de Verdiguier from 1765 to 1781, is the largest and most representative, having become a symbol of the city.

Another inheritance from Moorish times are the ruins of the mills which stand by the waterside around the bridge. The Molino de la Albolafia is the most interesting of these: its wheel channelled water along an

Plaza de los Capuchinos.

ingeniously-designed aqueduct to the former palace of the Emirs, located on the site of what is now the Episcopal Palace. However, the wheel visitors now see is not the original as its noise disturbed Queen Isabella the Catholic when she was in residence in the nearby Alcázar, and she ordered it dismantled.

Opposite the mosque, adjoining the Episcopal Palace, was installed in 1987, after the restoration of the 16th-century former Hospital of San Sebastián, the Palacio de Congresos y Exposiciones. This is the finest noble palace in the zone. It has a fine main front, popularly known as the Portada de San Jacinto, an exponent of the Gothic style with Plateresque influences.

The Jewish quarter also contains other noble buildings, such as what is now the faculty of Philosophy and Letters, occupying the former Hospital of Cardenal Salazar, also known as Hospital of los Agudos, built in the early-18th century and a jewel of the architecture of the Enlightenment. Adjoining this site is the Chapel of San Bartolomé, a Gothic-Mudéjar hermitage. Of the *Casa del Indiano* in Calle Fernández Ruano, only the original 15th-century façade is conserved, the ground floor built in Mudéjar style and the first floor in Isabelline.

Other houses of singular interest can be found in La Axerquía district, adjoining the Jewish quarter and also medieval. It is reached through the Arco del Portillo, an entrance opened in the inner walls of the city in the 14th century to communicate the «Almedina» with the «Axerquía», that is, the high and low districts of the city. In Calle de la Feria is the Palace of Los Marqueses del Carpio, a 16th-century noble mansion now restored in neo-Mudéjar style and featuring a tower from the old city walls.

The Cristo de los Faroles.

The Palace of the Páez de Castillejo family, now the seat of the city's Archaeological Museum, presides over Plaza de Jerónimo Páez. Nearby is the Palace of Los Fernández de Mesa, a 16th-century construction, and the Conservatory, also 16th-century, which possesses the best-preserved Plateresque façade in Córdoba. The headquarters of the Círculo de la Amistad, in Calle Alfonso XIII, is an important artistic and literary centre founded in the mid-19th century. The original building, dating to the 15th century, was first a hospital and later a convent. It possesses magnificent patios and an interesting collection of drawings and paintings by various artists. The main room contains various canvases alluding to the history of Córdoba. Further on, in Plazuela de Orive, is the Orive House or House of Los Villalones, featuring a harmonious Renaissance front by Hernán Ruiz I. Exploring the streets of Córdoba, the visitor discovers such a number of lovely spots that it would be impossible to enumerate them all here. The picturesque confronts us in so many of its streets, squares and gardens, presided over, in many cases, by statues of illustrious Cordobans: in Plaza de las Capuchinas is that of Bishop Osio (257-357), advisor to Constantine

Plaza de las Tendillas.

High-Speed Train (AVE) station.

Avenida del Gran Capitán.

the Great; a monument to the great Spanish poet Luis de Góngora (1561-1627) stands in Plaza de la Trinidad; whilst the Romantic poet Angel de Saavedra, Duke of Rivas (1791-1865), author of «Don Alvaro o la fuerza del sino», is immortalised in the Jardines de la Victoria; in the Jewish quarter we find, in Plazuela de Tiberiades, a monument to Maimonides (1135-1205), the famous Jewish philosopher and doctor. Another native of Córdoba was the great bullfighter Manuel Rodríguez, «Manolete», (1917-1947). The son and grandson of bullfighters, he first entered the ring in Córdoba in 1939, establishing himself as a leading figure in the art of tauromachy. Due to his courage and professional honour, Manolete became a legendary figure, reinforced by his death in the bullring in Linares, gored by the bull «Islero».

One of the most impressive squares in Córdoba is,

without a doubt, Plaza de los Capuchinos, also known as Plaza de los Dolores or del Cristo de los Faroles («of the Christ of the Lamps»). The square is of great simplicity and surprises due to its silence. In the centre, like an abandoned processional *paso* (float), is the statue of El Cristo de los Faroles, its name alluding to the lamps which, in the form of iron flowers, reverently illuminate this representation of the Crucifixion. The statue was placed here in 1794, since when it has been the subject of pious popular devotion. On the left-hand side of the square is the 17th-century Capuchins' Convent, whilst on the right is the Hospital of San Jacinto, founded in 1596, adjoining the Church of Los Dolores, built in the 18th century. This peaceful church contains one of the statutes most revered by the faithful of Córdoba, that of the Virgin of Los Dolores, carved by the Granada-born

Roman temple.

sculptor Juan Prieto in 1719. It is the custom of young brides to offer this Virgin a dozen eggs on their wedding day.

Plaza de las Tendillas, presided over by the monument to «El Gran Capitán», now forms the urban heart of the city, and is a popular meeting-point for locals and visitors alike. This is a spacious, dynamic square and even in Roman times was the focal point of the city, though its present structure corresponds to the beginning of this century. Crowning one of the buildings lining the square, a peculiar clock denies the tragic nature of the passing of time, chiming it out to the sound of Flamenco music each quarter of an hour. If Plaza de las Tendillas is the liveliest square in Córdoba, Plaza de la Corredera is the most popular and picturesque. This square is what is known as «Castilian» in style, and is the only one of its kind in Andalusia. Its present structure dates back to the late-17th century, though it also conserves various older buildings, whose style contrasts sharply with the uniform surroundings. Built in brick and austerely decorated, Plaza de la Corredera was where events of various types, including, particularly, bullfights, took place. In the late-19th century it was converted into a covered market, but the iron framework was removed in 1959 and the square restored to its original appearance. The square currently accommodates the stalls of a small market, its stalls offering their varied wares whilst sheltered under the arcades are bars traditional inns and taverns.

A Cordoban patio.

THE PATIOS OF CORDOBA

The Cordoban patios make up one of the most charming attractions of the city and, moreover, represent a unique tradition in the world, as they are based on the Cordoban way of life. These are courtyards which, be they aristocratic or be they popular, are always original, clean, as refreshing as an oasis in the desert, and full of plants and flowers.

The origins of the Cordoban patio go back to Roman times, when houses were arranged around an open space used as an *agora,* and to the Moorish period when, although the palaces and cities had their own patios, the model of the Roman house continued to be followed, with the addition of flowerbeds and water in the shape of a well or fountain. The Cordoban patio was, then, an *agora* for the Romans and a *casinillo* for the Moors.

The patios communicate directly with the rooms and galleries of the houses, either through windows and balconies or through graceful arcades. The walls surrounding them are often literally covered with flowers and climbing plants. Fruit trees and flowers of all kinds, spreading their perfume everywhere, give a colourful air to this perpetual *fiesta* and create a miracle of peace under leafy shadows in the heart of the city.

The houses of the Jewish quarter are characterised by their narrow fronts and deep interiors. Their entrance porch and lack of many windows, maintaining

A typical patio in Calle Cardenal Herrero.

the privacy of the household, are typical of the Moorish culture. The magnificent wrought iron work of the grilles over doors and windows allow us to catch a glimpse of the shady canopy over the multi-coloured flora of the Cordoban patio.

Besides their floral exuberance, these patios also feature the ornamental presence of murmuring fountains, poetic waterspouts, lovely ceramic pieces, artistic wrought iron work, graceful porches, elegant tiles and, everywhere, the shiny brilliance of white-wash, unifying colours and softening angles.

The Cordoban patio is present both in the great mansions of the city and in more modest dwellings, but its fundamental character -within, obviously, great differences as regards architecture, space or sumptuousness- is the same in a humble house as in a great palace. The patio of the most modest house in Córdoba is rich in flowers and generous in shade, water and whitewash, creating an atmosphere of peace in which there is no room for bad taste. These popular patios are tiny, charming gardens which, situated in the centre of the houses, inundate them with joy and unfettered beauty.

At number 50, Calle San Basilio, not far from the Alcázar gardens, is the home of the Association of Friends of the Cordoban Patios. Its own patio is a good example of the communal courtyard, white-washed and abundant, above all, in flower pots.

A typical patio in Calle Basilio.

Two views of the patio of the Convent of Santa Marta. The patios of Córdoba are characterised by the presence of water, whether in the form of a well or a fountain.

A Cordoban patio.

The association is dedicated to the work of rehabilitating old houses, remodelling and restoring their patios.

As for aristocratic patios, there are many of these, in a wide variety of styles, in Córdoba. Like their popular cousins, all have their interest and strong personality. But we can, perhaps, mention particularly those of the Palacio de Los Marqueses de Viana, twelve in total, as well as gardens, for not for nothing is this palace known as the Patio Museum. The entrance patio goes back to the 17th century and is beautifully adorned, as are the others, with abundant orange trees, cypresses, fountains, flowers... Overall a veritable paradise. Other lovely exponents of the aristocratic patio include those of the Bishop's Palace or those of the Círculo de la Amistad.

The best time of year to enjoy the splendour of these patios is during the Cordoban patio competition, which takes place during the May Festivals. This is a unique occasion, as the residents open the gates of their houses and allow visitors into their patios. The patio competition takes place during the second and, sometimes, third, weekends in May. Each year, some 40 patios are opened to allow the public to appreciate their beauty, and to com-

An aristocratic Cordoban patio.

Patios of the more popular type often feature flowery trellises. ▷

pete for first prize. To visit them during the day and then to attend some of the different events which take place in the evening, such as Flamenco concerts, is a unique experience.

The May Festivals are of great importance within the rich folklore of Córdoba. The fiesta begins in the patio but spreads into the street. In the Fiesta de la Cruz, the streets and squares of the city are decked with splendid May Crosses, which also compete for beauty. The rich and varied cultural origins of the city give way to a vast diversity of folkloric events during these Festivals, districts vying with each other over the decoration of their patios and organising merry feasts which, though begun in intimacy, soon burst out onto the streets and into the squares. Wine -Montilla and Moriles- flows, feet tap out dance steps and heartfelt *soleás* are sung by lusty throats.

Parallel to the Festival de los Patios, Córdoba also hosts -in the Alcázar gardens, in the ring of Plaza de la Corredera and at many other fine venues- performances of Flamenco music, classical music concerts, ballet, theatre and *cante jondo* competitions.

A Cordoban patio.

Patio de las Columnas in the Palacio de Viana.

The patio of the bishop's house.

Patio de la Cancela in the Palacio de Viana. There are a total of twelve patios in the grounds of this palace, all different all lovely, making the site a «patio museum», as it is often known.

CHRISTIAN CHURCHES

After the reconquest of the city by Ferdinand III, the Holy, in 1236 and the consecration of the mosque as a cathedral, fourteen parish churches and various convents were founded in the city, their construction taking place between the late-13th and early-14th centuries. Also known as *Fernandinas,* these churches contain Romanesque and Gothic elements with touches of the Mudéjar in the architectural style, though many were later lined in baroque style.

Among these Christian churches, outstanding are those of San Nicolás de la Villa, featuring elegant tower and the peculiarity of square apses; San Miguel, which has a fine side door bearing influences of the Caliphal style; San Pedro, rebuilt in the 16th century, its new front designed by Hernán Ruiz II; San Pablo, which contains various magnificent Mudéjar-style chapels and the sculptural group of «Nuestra Señora de las Angustias», a masterpiece of Spanish imagery by the Cordoban artist Juan de Mesa; the Church of San Andrés, now greatly altered from its original state, built over the site of a Mozarabic church devoted to Saint Zoilo; La Magdalena, with three trumpet-shaped portals with semicircular arches, one of them Mudéjar in style; the Church of San Lorenzo, characterised by the porch before the main entrance, an infrequent element in Andalusian religious architecture; and the Church of Santa Marina, with its fortress-like aspect. The Church of San Francisco was, before it was secularised, the Convent of San Pedro el Real, founded by Ferdinand III, the Holy. Part of its medieval cloisters can still be admired here. The Church of La Trinidad, dating to the 18th century, consists of a single nave. Finally, the Church of San Rafael was built in neoclassical style in the early-19th century in honour of the city's guardian archangel. The interior contains a fine polychrome sculpture of Raphael by Gómez de Sandoval in 1795.

Church of Santa Marina de Aguas Santas and the monument to the bullfighter Manolete.

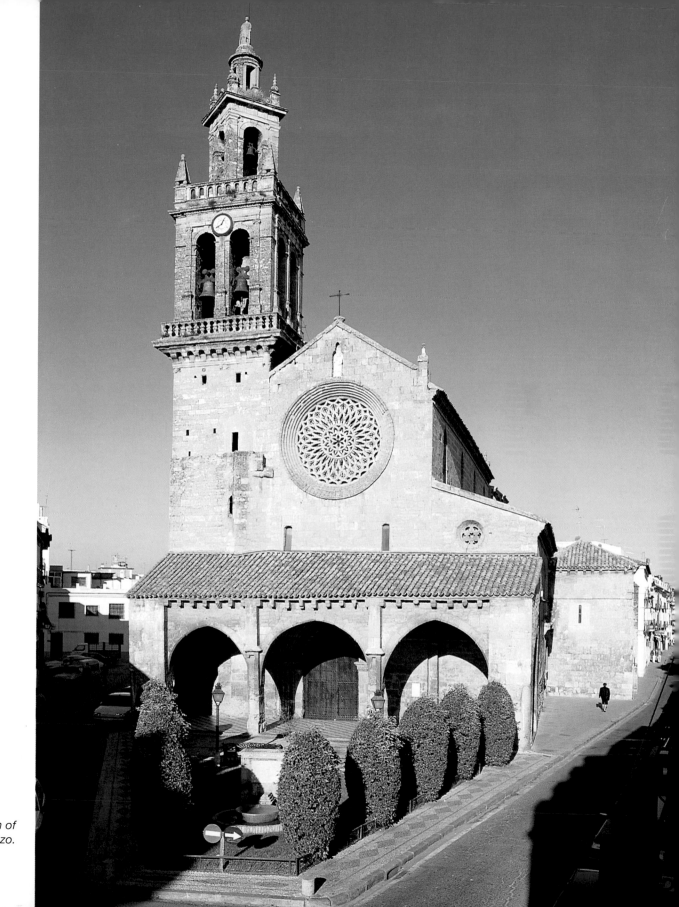

*Church of
San Lorenzo.*

Statue of
the Virgin
in her niche
during the
festivities
of Holy
Week.

The Cristo del Remedio de Animas.

A view of Holy Week in Córdoba. ▷

HOLY WEEK

Holy Week in Córdoba, as throughout Andalusia, is celebrated with great splendour. On the afternoon of Good Friday, mass is held in the mosque, accompanied by a symphony orchestra and large choir. The processions, bearing their artistic *pasos,* floats, parade around the cathedral and the picturesque winding streets of the surrounding area. Among the images taking part in the processions, of outstanding beauty are those of Nuestra Señora de los Dolores, El Cristo del Remedio de Animas, El Cristo del Rescatado and El Cristo de la Misericordia.

*The Church of San
Andrés.*

*The Church of San
Francisco.*

*The Church of San
Pedro.*

Plaza del Potro.

PLAZA DEL POTRO

The Plaza del Potro is one of the most evocative corners of Córdoba, a spacious rectangular-shaped square of the city full of tradition, harmonious architecture and, at the same time, great warmth. During the 15th and 16th centuries it was the meeting-point for merchants and travellers from all over the Peninsula, the refuge of rogues and a labour exchange. Its present name was given to it in 1577, when the famous fountain was installed here, crowned by a rearing *potro* (colt) bearing the coat of arms of the city. To one side of the square is the Posada del Potro, conserved almost intact since the time when it was immortalised by Cervantes in his *Don Quijote* and *Rinconete and Cortadillo*. This is an outstanding example of 16th-century housing, very common at the time, known as «Corrales», various houses arranged around a courtyard with a well. The Posada del Potro has now been converted into a cultural and exhibition centre.

At one end of the square is a new triunfo de San Rafael, whilst on the other, opposite the Posada del Potro, is the medieval building of the former Hospital de la Caridad, now seat of the Julio Romero de Torres and Fine Art museums.

Plaza del Potro: front of the Museum of Fine Art and that dedicated to Julio Romero de Torres.

Julio Romero de Torres' female portraits transmit great sensuality.

JULIO ROMERO DE TORRES MUSEUM

The Julio Romero de Torres Museum is one of the most popular in the city in terms of numbers of visitors, drawn here by the personality and artistry of this great Cordoban painter. This museum and house has over 50 of Romero's works, as well as furniture and many of the artist's personal effects, photographs and portraits by contemporary artists, such as the bust of Romero by Mariano Benlliure. After his death, the work of this inspired painter was donated to the city by his family, after which the museum was created.

The work of Julio Romero de Torres (1874-1930) is inspired in the artist's native Córdoba and takes as its main theme the female figure, outstandingly portraits of Gypsy women full of sensuality. Romero was a very successful and popular painter in his time, often causing controversy due to the theme of many of his works. «La Chiquita Piconera», «Oranges and Lemons», «Sin», «Poem to Córdoba», «Viva el Pelo», «Trini's Granddaughter» and «Homage to the Art of Bullfighting» are just a few of the interesting works by this «painter of dark women», as the popular song calls him.

The work of Julio Romero de Torres takes its inspiration from the Córdoba where he was born.

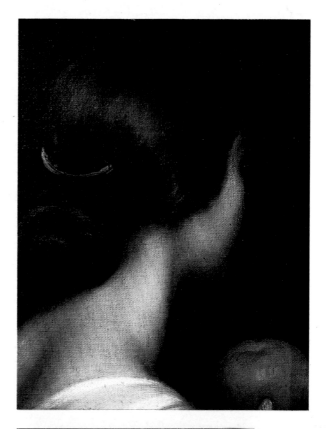

The female figure and, particularly, Cordoban women, is a central theme of the work of Julio Romero de Torres.

«*Homage to the art of bullfighting*», *a painting by Julio Romero de Torres.*

Fragment of «*The poem of Córdoba*», *one of the most outstanding works by Julio Romero de Torres.*

The Fine Arts Museum has various collections, including one of late-medieval painting.

FINE ART MUSEUM

A small gardened patio adorned with sculptures from different periods forms the antechamber to the two museums, the Fine Art Museum and that dedicated to Julio Romero de Torres, which share the medieval building of the former Hospital de la Caridad. The former occupies, basically, the former church of the hospital, as well as various other rooms.

Opened in 1862, this museum contains works by such artists as Pedro Romana, Valdés Leal, Antonio del Castillo, Eugenio Lucas, Pedro de Córdoba, Alejo Fernández, José de Saravia, Juan de Peñalosa, José Ignacio Cobo Guzmán, Rafael Romero Barros -father of Julio Romero de Torres- and the Romero de Torres brothers, amongst others. Contemporary artists represented include Pedro Botí and Pedro Bueno.

There is also an important collection of works by the Cordoban sculptor Mateo Inurria, as well as excellent engravings by Ricardo Baroja and Francisco Iturrino. Also interesting is the collection of drawings, including works by such artists as Ribera, García Reinoso and Antonio del Castillo.

Front of the Palace of Los Páez de Castillejo, which now houses the Archaeological Museum.

Curb of a Mudéjar well.

ARCHAEOLOGICAL MUSEUM

The Archaeological Museum is housed in the former Palace of the Páez de Castillejo family in Plaza Jerónimo Páez. This palace has a lovely portal, though now much deteriorated, designed by Hernán Ruiz and the sculptors Francisco Jato and Francisco Linares, dating back to the 16th century. Inside, the museum collections are organised around rooms and patios to form an itinerary containing pieces from a period ranging from prehistoric times to the medieval epoch. In short, sumptuous staircases, rich coffering and lovely aristocratic patios make a visit to this museum -one of the most important of its kind in Spain- a pure delight both due to the importance of its archaeological collections and the beauty of the building which houses them.

The collections comprise a veritable historical archive of archaeology in the province, including pieces from the Neolithic Age, with findings from the terraces of the Guadalquivir and Guadaljoz rivers; many items from the Iberian period, such as vases, fibulae or lions and other animals evoking the protective gods; an important collection of mosaics, sculptures and other vestiges of Roman art, including a magnificent statue of Mithra and another of Minerva in white marble; and a large range of items from the Visigoth period. Particularly complete and important is the collection of artistic objects dating back to Moorish times:

Bronze stag from Medina Azahara. ▷

Roman mosaic from Valenzoleja.

Early Christian sarcophagus.

Iberian lion found in Carteia.

Silver Moorish coins.

statues, coffins, fonts, capitals, glass and silverwork, the latter featuring an inlaid bronze stag recovered from a fountain in the Medina Azahara and a unique collection of pitchers decorated in Mudéjar style. The museum also has a fine collection of coins from all periods, as well as rooms dedicated to Renaissance and baroque art, including the original models used by Michel de Verdiguier to carve the cathedral pulpits.

Torre de la Calahorra.

CALAHORRA TOWER

The Torre de la Calahorra we can now contemplate dates to the year 1369, having been built during the reign of Henry II, though its name, meaning «free castle», reveals the Moorish origins of this fortress. It formerly consisted of two towers joined by an arch giving access to the city. It was declared a monument of historic and artistic interest in 1931 and since 1987 has housed a museum sponsored by the Roger Garaudy Foundation and devoted to the history of Córdoba during its period of greatest splendour, from the 9th to the 13th centuries, when this tolerant city saw the peaceful co-existence of Moors, Jews and Christians. This is an audiovisual museum in which the different models and reproductions are complemented by the voices of different historical personages. The terrace of the Torre de la Calahorra, moreover, commands magnificent views of the city and surrounding countryside to the south.

DIOCESAN MUSEUM

Opposite the mosque, in Calle Torrijos, is the former Episcopal Palace, now the seat of the Diocesan Museum. The building dates back to the 16th century and is arranged around an arcaded patio, but before being completely reformed was the residence of the Visigoth governors and alcázar to the caliphs. It was donated to the diocese after the Christian reconquest. The Diocesan Museum was opened in 1989 and contains an important artistic heritage belonging to the Cordoban church, from medieval times to our days. Collections of paintings, sculptures, tapestries, books, furniture and other objects may all be admired here. One of the rooms is dedicated to all the bishops of Córdoba from 1238 to the present, exhibiting their portraits. On the ground floor is the old palace chapel, featuring five baroque altarpieces.

PALACIO DE VIANA

The site of this palace-museum, registered as a National Artistic and Historic Monument and Artistic Garden, covers a total area of 6,500 m². This was a lordly mansion which belonged to various families over time, being extended by the construction of adjoining houses. Overall, this is a generally austere monument in which various architectural styles can be observed, from the 14th century to the present day. The main entrance, in Plaza de Don Gome, is attributed to Juan de Ochoa and dates to the 16th century, as does the magnificent main staircase. A visit to this palace is fully justified only by the sight of the exquisite gardens and 12 patios.

The different rooms in the building, conserving the atmosphere of the period, contain a wide and extensive range of art works: tapestries, paintings, jewellery, porcelain services, furniture, carpets, musical instruments, etc. There is also a complete collection of embossed and Cordoban leather goods, as well as an extensive library, rich, particularly, in books on hunting.

Sculpture of Ferdinand III, the Holy, who conquered the city of Córdoba in 1236.

Near the Palacio de Viana, in Calle Muñoz Capilla, is the Salvador Morera House Museum, a typical 17th-century Cordoban dwelling reconstructed by the author Salvador Morera. Inside are impressive ceramic murals, stained-glass pieces, iron sculptures and a fine collection of oil paintings.

Medieval tapestry.

THE ETHNOBOTANICAL MUSEUM

Situated on the right bank of the Guadalquivir, next to the Puente de San Rafael, the Ethnobotanical Museum was inaugurated in 1992. An educational institution, it recreates a universe which will please experts and the uninitiated alike. The main building contains the offices, a library and permanent exhibition rooms where different forms of the relations between people and plants can be studied. The museum also has various pavilions for tropical and desert plants, a rosegarden and a greenhouse divided into different microclimates where species characteristic of each are cultivated. All around these buildings are extensive gardens with trees and local flora, plants used for food, aromatic plants, ornamental plants and species in danger of extinction.

TAURINE MUSEUM

This peculiar museum occupies a 16th-century mansion known as the «Casa de las Bulas» in Plazuela de Maimónides in the heart of the Jewish quarter. Its rooms communicating with lovely patios, contain collections of diverse objects and mementoes of Cordoban bullfighters, particularly those who passed into history as «caliphas» of the art of tauromachy: Lagartijo, Guerrita and Manolete, as well as the rejoneador Antonio Cañero.
The museum also contains material and documents dating back to the 18th and 19th centuries, as well as information about bullfighters little known today but who were leading figures of their times, including Cerrajitas, Pegote and Panchón. The Taurine Museum also has a cultural programme, organising conferences and seminars, discussions about bullfighting and other activities related to the *fiesta nacional.*

CORDOBA AND BULLFIGHTING

The Córdoba school forms, with those of Seville and Ronda, the great trio of Andalusian bullfighting schools. The art of tauromachy is deeply-rooted in Córdoba,

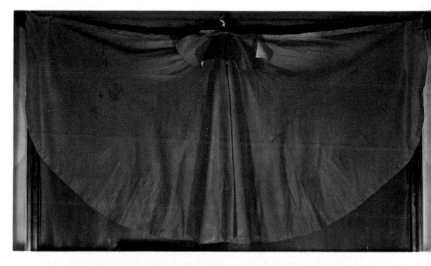

and the Santa Marina district of the city was where many great matadores were born. Córdoba has given the world a long list of illustrious bullfighters.

The bullring in Córdoba is known as «Los Califas» and stands in Gran Vía Parque. It is one of the seven first category rings in Spain. The *Feria Taurina* takes place here towards the end of May each year, coinciding with the *Feria de la Salud.* The *tienta,* a picturesque and daring *fiesta* in which the mettle of young bulls is put to the test, is another attractive event in the calendar of Cordoban folklore.

Old poster in the Taurine Museum.

Office of Lagartijo el Grande, in the Taurine Museum.

Torre de la Malmuerta.

TORRE DE LA MALMUERTA

This tower stands at one end of Plaza de Colón. Its structure is in stark contrast to the surrounding high buildings and wide avenues. Very well conserved, according to the inscriptions under the arch of this tower, it was built between 1406 and 1408 by order of Henry III of Castile.

Though its origins are unknown, its fortress-like aspect indicate that it perhaps formed part of the old city walls. Its name («Tower of the Wrongly Killed») refers to a popular legend of a nobleman who killed his wife, accusing her of adultery. Apprised of her innocence, he begged pardon of the king and was condemned to built the tower in memory of «La Malmuerta».

The construction of the tower is in the Moorish tradition, with octagonal shape and thick walls. It features such Mudéjar elements as the belt of fine carving supporting the battlements.

PALACIO DE LA DIPUTACION

Situated in spacious Plaza de Colón, the Palace of the Provincial Government represents the finest exponent of baroque art to be found in the city. Formerly a Convent of the Mercedarians, it is also known still by that name, though it was completely rebuilt in the 18th century and again altered later to house the Diputación Provincial.

The building features a broad front of bright colours and, inside, a lovely main staircase, as well as various patios, one of which, in Renaissance style, is particularly charming.

The Church of La Merced has a majestic portal dating to 1745 and contains various interesting paintings and a magnificent altarpiece with sculptures by Gómez Sandoval, though this is presently being restored after being damaged by fire.

Convent of La Merced, now seat of the provincial government.

Cordoban handcrafts in the narrow streets of the Jewish quarter.

CORDOBAN FOLKLORE

In the Jewish quarter and throughout the historic areas of the city in general are many taverns, traditional and typical in Córdoba, as well as souvenir and art shops. The Zoco provides, in fact, a splendid opportunity for the visitor to become familiar with the rich Cordoban artisanal traditions, in which the principal activities are silverwork (this is the land of silversmiths) and embossed leather.

Regarding local festivities, the month of May is the festive month *par excellence*. It begins with the Fiesta de la Cruz, a tradition celebrated by *peñas, cofradías* and other groups of residents who deck out streets, squares and other nooks with crosses made from flowers and other decorative elements. In the city itself, the council organises a competition for these May crosses, attracting around 80 entries each year. On the first Sunday in May, the Romería de Linares takes place. This is a religious procession to the Sanctuary containing the statue of the Virgin of Linares, a few kilometres from Córdoba, and commemorates the conquest of the city by Ferdinand the Holy, as legend has it that he brought with him a statue of this virgin. Next in May is the Cordoban Patio Competition, described above, which follows on from or coincides with the *Feria of Nuestra Señora de la Salud,* a fair which takes place during the last week of the month.

The *Feria de la Salud* is Córdoba's most important festivity. In the Arenal district, near the Guadalquivir, *casetas* -stands- are set up, and the fun begins.

Music, singing and dancing, wine, traditional costume and fairground attractions are the main protagonists in this warm, merry *fiesta* where, unlike the Seville and Jerez fairs, the *casetas* are open to all. Also on the programme during the fair are important corridas at Los Califas Bullring.

Both during the Feria de la Salud and on the day of the Virgin of La Fuensanta (co-patron saint of the city, her feast day being 8 September), visitors and locals alike can admire the dexterity of the horsemen of Córdoba as they trot their fine steeds around the streets of the city, alone or accompanied by beautiful Cordoban women. The «Velá» (vigil) of La Fuensanta takes place in the proximity of the Sanctuary of La Fuensanta, where the image of the saint has been venerated since the Middle Ages. On this day, it is the custom to buy a pottery bell and admire the so-called «caimán de la Fuensanta», a votive offering placed on the wall of the church which is surrounded by many legends. On 24 October, the city celebrates another fiesta, that of Saint Raphael, Córdoba's guardian archangel. On this feast day, it is traditional to make the journey to the nearby sierra and eat a «perol», a rice dish with meat.

Cordoban folklore.

A typical Cordoban dish is guisado de rabo de toro, bull's tail stew.

CORDOBAN GASTRONOMY

We are pleased to be able to report that the local taverns conserve their traditional virtues. These are normally quiet, peaceful places, where Cordobans meet to drink wine -especially fino- play dominoes or chat at midday or at the end of the working day. Whilst the more classical taverns do not serve food, these days many do provide tapas or «raciones» of gastronomic specialities.

Cordobans drink their wine with elegant sensuality. Whites from Montilla or Moriles, made using methods similar to those employed for Jerez sherry, aromatic, golden wine of exquisite bouquet, the unison of the senses with the spirit.

Among the most typical local dishes are the *salmorejo*, a sauce similar to a thick gazpacho which can be eaten with a spoon or with bread, fried aubergine and bull's tail. Various culinary traditions meet in Córdoba: the Moorish influence can be detected in sweetmeats such as *alfarjores* and *Pastel Cordobés,* this last a cake made from pastry, whilst the *guiso con habas secas* (a bean stew) and gazpacho are dishes left by the Jews. And all over the province of Córdoba, tasty game dishes are available, for this is rich hunting land. Also popular are the local dishes using fresh fish brought from the nearby sea.

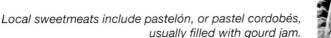

Local sweetmeats include pastelón, or pastel cordobés, usually filled with gourd jam.

During the Fiesta de la Cross, which takes place in May, the streets are decorated with crosses made from flowers, always accompanied by plants and other floral elements.

Aerial view of Medina Azahara.

MEDINA AZAHARA

Some eight kilometres from the city centre, at the foot of the so-called Monte de la Desposada, are the ruins of the palace city of Madinat al-Zahra, or Medina Azahara, a symbol of Córdoba's illustrious Caliphal past considered the «Versailles of Moorish Art».

The life of this magnificent architectural site, made up of a walled area of 1,125 hectares, was as splendid as it was brief. Construction began in 936 under Abderramán III, first Caliph of Al-Andalus, apparently in honour of his favourite, Al Zahra. The work took some 25 years to complete, with no expense or effort spared. Contemporary chroniclers claim that the pal-

ace rested on 1,000 marble columns and that its walls were lined with gold, as well as mentioning the best architects from Baghdad and Constantinople as working here. However, just 74 years later, in 1010, the Medina Azahara was completely sacked and burnt down by Berbers in the course of the Fitna, or civil war which led to the Caliphate being broken up into taifas, small kingdoms. Later, moreover, its fountains, columns, stones and capitals were taken away for use in the building of churches and palaces.

The Medina Azahara was the court and palace of the caliphs Abderramán III, his son Alhakem II, who carried out a number of alterations, and the successor to the latter, Hixén II. Hixén II, however, was supplanted by the minister Almanzor, who imprisoned him in the Medina Azahara, devoted to studying the Koran, building the Medina Al-Zahira as the centre of the administrative structure of the caliphate.

The city of Medina Azahara was structured in terraces which adapted to the form of the sierra, and could hold up to 12,000 people. The higher section was occupied by palaces, whilst in the middle were gardens and vegetable plots, green spaces separating the court proper from the lower part of the city where, huddled around the main mosque, were the houses of those who worked in the complex or in the workshops, or as guards to the citadel.

In 1910, work began on the archaeological excavation of the site, an arduous work of reconstruction which has allowed a number of rooms to be opened up to permit visitors a glimpse of the decorative wealth of this fabulous city, reflecting the sumptuousness of the Medina Azahara during its period of splendour. The «Salón Rico», formerly the reception room, is now largely restored. It consists of three naves opening up to a transversal entrance porch. The columns are in alternately blue and red marble with Caliphal marble capitals. The voussoirs of the arches are magnificently decorated, as are the upper socles, which feature fine ornamental work using floral motifs. More of the legacy left by the Medina Azahara, particularly everyday objects such as vases, ornaments and ceramic plates, can been seen in the Archaeological Museum in Córdoba itself.

Two views of the restoration of the Medina Azahara palace and city.

*Various examples of the fine workmanship apparent in
the remains unearthed from the ruins of Medina Azahara.*

«Cypress Avenue», as it is known, at the site of the Cordoban hermitages.

THE HERMITAGES

The hermitages of Córdoba stand amidst the singular and lovely landscape of the foothills of the Sierra Morena, some 20 kilometres from the city. Though their origins go back to the time of Moorish domination, the present hermitages were built between 1703 and 1709, as at first the hermits lived in isolation and it was not until the late-17th century that Brother Francisco Jesús decided that all should join together to live in the same place and that the church, finally completed in the middle of the following century, should be built. Since 1957, the hermitages have been under the administration of the Order of Descalced Carmelites.

The site is presided over by a spectacular monument to the Sacred Heart of Jesus, by Coullant Valera in 1929. The recondite paths, lined by cypress trees, the whitewashed cells of the monks and the austere cemetery, as well as the splendid views over the city and surrounding countryside, all combine to give this spot a particular charm.

At night, the Cristo de los Faroles acquires particular beauty.

CORDOBA BY NIGHT

To explore Córdoba by the light of the moon is to undertake a lovely, unforgettable adventure of the spirit, a unique, surprising sensual and aesthetic pleasure. Strolling the streets of the Jewish quarter, or down to the banks of the Guadalquivir, we feel we are living in a magical world. History seems present, timeless, shining in the Cordoban night in all the most picturesque nooks of the city. Particularly attractive is the «Virgen de los Faroles» in the north wall of the mosque, and the «Cristo de los Faroles» in the silent Plaza de los Capuchinos.

The nocturnal peace and quiet of many of the streets and squares of Córdoba contrasts with the atmosphere when the city is celebrating its *fiestas*, for during the Feria de la Salud or other festivities, the night is filled with song and dance. And though the city is small, it offers much in the way of cultural events, and not just at night. One of the main focusses of culture here is the Gran Teatro, with a permanent programme of drama, music and dance, whilst the Teatro de la Axerquía, recently reorganised, stages magnificent open-air performances.

The cathedral-mosque and the Roman bridge seem to be watched over by the Archangel Raphael in this work by Bernabé Gómez del Río (1651).

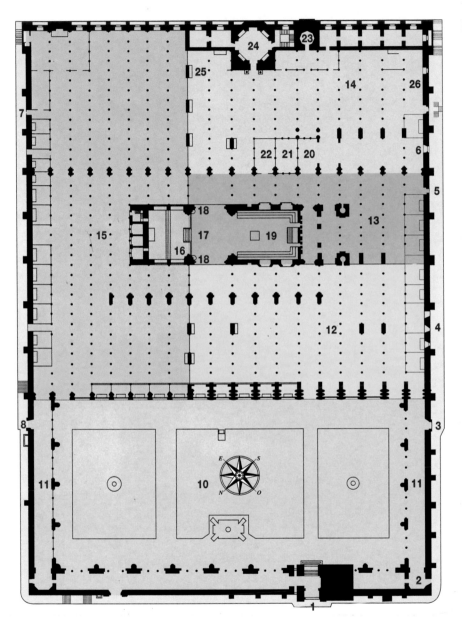

PLAN OF THE MOSQUE

1. Puerta del Perdón.
2. Postigo de la Leche.
3. Puerta de los Deanes.
4. Puerta de San Esteban.
5. Puerta de San Miguel.
6. Postigo de Palacio.
7. Postigo del Sagrario.
8. Puerta de Santa Catalina.
9. Puerta de las Palmas.
10. Courtyard of the Oranges.
11. Cloister.
12. Aisles of Abderramán I.
13. Extension of Abderramán II.
14. Extension of Al-Hakam II.
15. Aisles of Almanzor.
16. Capilla Mayor.
17. Transept.
18. Pulpits.
19. Coro.
20. Chapel of Villaviciosa.
21. Capilla Real.
22. Chapel of San Pablo.
23. *Mihrab*.
24. Chapel of Santa Teresa and Treasure.
25. Last Supper.
26. Visigoth Museum of San Vicente.

Collection ALL EUROPE

	Spanish	French	English	German	Italian	Catalan	Dutch	Swedish	Portuguese	Japanese	Finnish
1 ANDORRA	•	•	•	•		•					
2 LISBON	•	•	•	•					•		
3 LONDON	•	•	•	•						•	
4 BRUGES	•	•	•	•			•				
5 PARIS	•	•	•	•						•	
6 MONACO	•	•	•	•	•						
7 VIENNA	•	•	•	•							
11 VERDUN	•	•	•	•			•				
12 THE TOWER OF LONDON	•	•	•								
13 ANTWERP		•	•				•				
14 WESTMINSTER ABBEY	•	•	•	•							
15 THE SPANISH RIDING SCHOOL IN VIENNA	•	•	•	•							
16 FATIMA	•	•	•	•					•		
17 WINDSOR CASTLE	•	•	•	•							
19 COTE D'AZUR	•	•	•	•							
22 BRUSSELS	•	•	•	•			•				
23 SCHÖNBRUNN PALACE	•	•	•	•							
24 ROUTE OF PORT WINE	•	•	•	•							
26 HOFBURG PALACE	•	•	•	•							
27 ALSACE	•	•	•	•			•				
31 MALTA		•	•	•							
32 PERPIGNAN		•									
33 STRASBOURG	•	•	•	•							
34 MADEIRA + PORTO SANTO		•	•	•					•		
35 CERDAGNE - CAPCIR		•				•					
36 BERLIN	•	•	•	•	•						

Collection ART IN SPAIN

	Spanish	French	English	German	Italian	Catalan	Dutch	Swedish	Portuguese	Japanese	Finnish
1 PALAU DE LA MUSICA CATALANA	•		•			•					
2 GAUDI	•	•	•	•						•	
3 PRADO MUSEUM I (Spanish Painting)	•	•	•	•						•	
4 PRADO MUSEUM II (Foreign Painting)	•	•	•	•						•	
5 MONASTERY OF GUADALUPE	•	•	•	•							
6 THE CASTLE OF XAVIER	•	•	•	•						•	
7 THE FINE ARTS MUSEUM OF SEVILLE	•	•	•	•							
8 SPANISH CASTLES	•	•	•	•							
9 THE CATHEDRALS OF SPAIN	•	•	•	•							
10 THE CATHEDRAL OF GIRONA	•	•	•			•					
11 GRAN TEATRO DEL LICEO	•	•	•			•					
11 EL LICEO ARDE DE NUEVO	•										
12 THE CATHEDRAL OF CORDOBA	•	•	•	•	•						
13 THE CATHEDRAL OF SEVILLE	•	•	•	•							
14 PICASSO	•	•	•	•						•	
15 REALES ALCAZARES (ROYAL PALACE OF SEVILLE)	•	•	•	•							
16 MADRID'S ROYAL PALACE	•	•	•	•							
17 ROYAL MONASTERY OF EL ESCORIAL	•	•	•	•							
18 THE WINES OF CATALONIA	•										
19 THE ALHAMBRA AND THE GENERALIFE	•	•	•	•							
20 GRANADA AND THE ALHAMBRA	•	•	•	•							
21 ROYAL ESTATE OF ARANJUEZ	•	•	•	•							
22 ROYAL ESTATE OF EL PARDO	•	•	•	•							
23 ROYAL HOUSES	•	•	•	•	•						
24 ROYAL PALACE OF SAN ILDEFONSO	•	•	•	•							
25 HOLLY CROSS OF THE VALLE DE LOS CAIDOS	•	•	•	•							
26 OUR LADY OF THE PILLAR OF SARAGOSSA	•	•	•	•							
27 TEMPLE DE LA SAGRADA FAMILIA	•	•	•	•		•					
28 POBLET ABTEI	•	•	•	•		•					
29 MAJORCA CATHEDRAL	•	•	•	•		•					

Collection ALL SPAIN

	Spanish	French	English	German	Italian	Catalan	Dutch	Swedish	Portuguese	Japanese	Finnish
1 ALL MADRID	•	•	•	•						•	
2 ALL BARCELONA	•	•	•	•						•	
3 ALL SEVILLE	•	•	•	•							
4 ALL MAJORCA	•	•	•	•							
5 ALL THE COSTA BRAVA	•	•	•	•							
6 ALL MALAGA and the Costa del Sol	•	•	•	•							
7 ALL THE CANARY ISLANDS (Gran Canaria)	•	•	•	•				•	•		
8 ALL CORDOBA	•	•	•	•				•			
9 ALL GRANADA	•	•	•	•							
10 ALL VALENCIA	•	•	•	•							
11 ALL TOLEDO	•	•	•	•							
12 ALL SANTIAGO	•	•	•	•							
13 ALL IBIZA and Formentera	•	•	•	•							
14 ALL CADIZ and the Costa de la Luz	•	•	•	•							
15 ALL MONTSERRAT	•	•	•	•							
16 ALL SANTANDER and Cantabria	•	•	•								
17 ALL THE CANARY ISLANDS II (Tenerife)	•	•	•	•				•	•		•
20 ALL BURGOS	•	•	•	•							
21 ALL ALICANTE and the Costa Blanca	•	•	•	•							
22 ALL NAVARRA	•	•	•	•							
23 ALL LERIDA	•	•	•			•					
24 ALL SEGOVIA	•	•	•	•							
25 ALL SARAGOSSA	•	•	•	•							
26 ALL SALAMANCA	•	•	•	•					•		
27 ALL AVILA	•	•	•	•							
28 ALL MINORCA	•	•	•	•							
29 ALL SAN SEBASTIAN and Guipúzcoa	•										
30 ALL ASTURIAS	•	•	•								
31 ALL LA CORUNNA and the Rías Altas	•	•	•								
32 ALL TARRAGONA	•	•	•	•							
33 ALL MURCIA	•	•	•								
34 ALL VALLADOLID	•	•	•	•							
35 ALL GIRONA	•	•	•	•		•					
36 ALL HUESCA	•	•	•	•							
37 ALL JAEN	•	•	•	•							
40 ALL CUENCA	•	•	•	•							
41 ALL LEON	•	•	•	•							
42 ALL PONTEVEDRA, VIGO and the Rías Bajas	•	•	•	•							
43 ALL RONDA	•	•	•	•							
44 ALL SORIA	•										
46 ALL EXTREMADURA	•	•	•	•							
47 ALL ANDALUSIA	•	•	•	•							
52 ALL MORELLA	•	•		•		•					

Collection ALL AMERICA

	Spanish	French	English	German	Italian	Catalan	Dutch	Swedish	Portuguese	Japanese	Finnish
1 PUERTO RICO	•	•									
2 SANTO DOMINGO	•	•									
3 QUEBEC		•	•								
4 COSTA RICA	•	•									
5 CARACAS	•	•									

Collection ALL AFRICA

	Spanish	French	English	German	Italian	Catalan	Dutch	Swedish	Portuguese	Japanese	Finnish
1 MOROCCO	•	•	•	•							
2 THE SOUTH OF MOROCCO	•	•	•	•							
3 TUNISIA		•	•	•							
4 RWANDA		•	•								

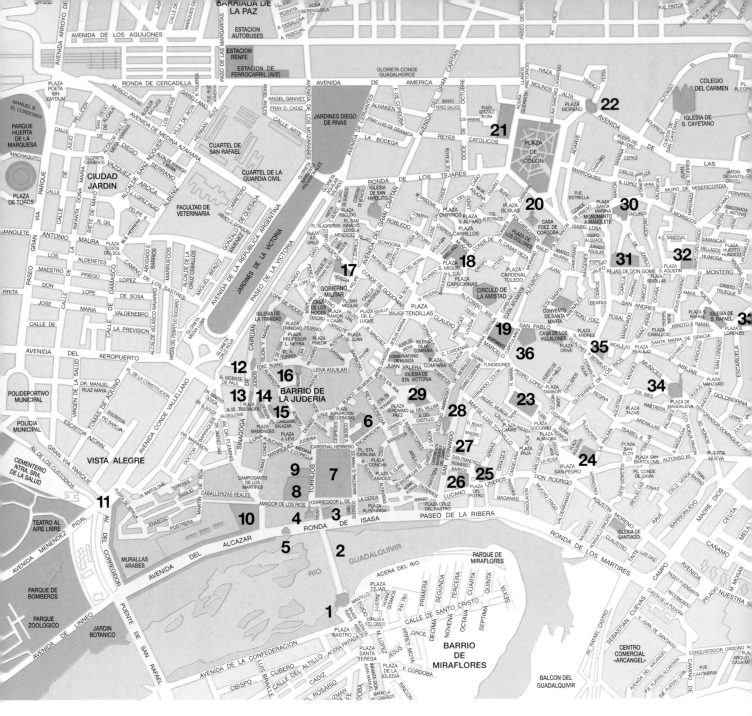

CORDOBA

1. Torre de la Calahorra
2. Puente Romano
3. Puerta del Puente
4. Triunfo de San Rafael
5. Molino de la Albolafia
6. Calleja de las Flores
7. Mezquita y Catedral
8. Palacio Episcopal
9. Portada de San Jacinto
10. Alcázar de los Reyes Cristianos
11. Puerta de Sevilla
12. Puerta de Almodóvar
13. Sinagoga
14. Museo Municipal Taurino
15. Capilla de San Bartolomé
16. Casa del Indiano
17. San Nicolás de la Villa
18. San Miguel
19. Templo Romano
20. Cristo de los Faroles
21. Palacio de la Diputación
22. Torre de la Malmuerta
23. Plaza de la Corredera
24. San Pedro
25. Museo Julio Romero de Torres y Museo de Bellas Artes
26. Posada del Potro
27. San Francisco
28. Arco del Portillo
29. Museo Arqueológico
30. Santa Marina de Aguas Santas
31. Palacio de Viana
32. San Agustín
33. San Lorenzo
34. La Magdalena
35. San Andrés
36. San Pablo